Tips, Ideas and Stories From Around the World

RICK FULTON

HR ANYWHERE: TIPS, IDEAS AND STORIES FROM AROUND THE WORLD

Copyright © 2021 by Rick Fulton

All rights reserved. Printed in the United States of America. No part of this book may be used or reproduced in any manner whatsoever without written permission except in the case of brief quotations embodied in critical articles or reviews.

For permissions contact: Rick Fulton at Rickefulton@gmail.com

ISBN: 979-8-5150810-0-3

First Edition: June 2021

Table of Contents

Rick Fulton: Bio i

Introduction iii

Chapter 1: What do I do NOW???? 1

Chapter 2: Local Recruiting and Training Plan 9

Chapter 3: Job Descriptions and Mobilizations 15

Chapter 4: Good Corporate Citizen 21

Chapter 5: Office Set-Up 23

Chapter 6: Policy and Procedures 25

Chapter 7: Recruiting and Hiring 29

Chapter 8: Onboarding 33

Chapter 9: Reporting 37

Chapter 10: HR Administration 41

Chapter 11: Demobilization 49

Chapter 12: Project End 51

Sample Templates 54

Rick Fulton: Bio

Rick Fulton is a new author with extensive experience in the Human Resource world, working globally in some of the most dangerous, austere, and remote environments.

There have been many times that Rick asked himself, "What on earth am I doing here?"

Normally, this would transpire when taking shelter in small concrete bunkers with several fellow co-workers, during mortar attacks in Iraq, or taking bucket baths in Africa and water bottle showers in Afghanistan.

Rick has had the unique distinction of working in some of the most difficult countries to live in such as Iraq, Afghanistan, Kazakhstan, and Guinea, along with Newfoundland Canada.

He is passionate about helping small-to-midsize HR teams enhance their skills to get Human Resource Departments back to treating humans the way they should be treated – like humans.

Rick also has a YouTube Channel covering HR issues and provides tips on how to become a Highly Esteemed HR Professional

As an HR professional, he feels blessed to have worked in some very unique environments, which is why he has a number of "war" stories that has transformed his skill set and belief that there are very few issues he has not been exposed to thus far. Not content with confining all this acquired skills to himself, he is also keen to throw light on some of these cases and share his experiences through the book and hopes you find it somewhat entertaining.

His website is:
www.globalhrc.net/
You can contact him at:
rickefulton@gmail.com

Introduction

How many times have you found yourself heading straight to a YouTube Channel to determine whether there is a step-by-step process to start something you are passionate about? Do you prefer reading a book like "Start-Up for Dummies?" Contrary to popular notion, this is a process many of us follow more often than not.

In my 30+ years of experience working for a heavy industrial Fortune 200 construction behemoth, each project felt like a new learning experience and there were very few takeaways from the previous one. Very often, a firm would provide very general procedures without offering specific details for guidance. It is like walking onto a project with a large whiteboard in front of you and having to develop new programs from scratch. Needless to say, this can be a very frustrating and daunting process.

In this book, I intend to help solve this problem by offering guidance that has been developed over 30 years in some of the very remote, austere, and dangerous environments such as Iraq, Afghanistan, Kazakhstan, and Guinea – as well as in the US and Canada. These guidelines are unique in that they are location/region-agnostic and can be easily implemented to start a successful HR Field Office, anywhere in the world, even in active war zones. You will also come across personal "war stories" that might help you better understand the need to take appropriate measures.

Once, a mentor of mine said he felt he could be dropped anywhere in the world and open an HR office professionally, efficiently, and most importantly, productively. Thanks to my learning experience from this HR guru along with many other respected HR professionals, I can do the same, and so can you. In fact, you can use the information offered by this book to become your firm's HR expert.

A caveat: the following chapters are not cookie-cutter steps as each project can entail different requirements based on geographic area, environment, cultures, and clients-specific needs. For example, you may not setup the same office in Baghdad, Iraq as you would in downtown New York City. This is because the two countries' cultures and national laws are as different as chocolate and peanut butter. As an HR professional, you must ensure you're not violating any local laws that could incite riots, which is not hard to do in some countries if you are not transparent in your approach and do not comply with local standards. Although most of my examples pertain to the construction industry, they could be extended to just about any business line. The construction industry is fluid and regularly sets up new locations. This allows many good examples to utilize on what to do and not do. I am happy to share my knowledge and experience.

It is my hopes to share some stories that reflect the challenges and flexibility that HR Professionals might deal with in any environment.

This was amply demonstrated in one of our mega projects in Guinea, West Africa. The mining project involved the extraction of arguably the world's purest Iron Ore. We needed to build a rail system extending from the Atlantic Ocean Coast line, inland 435 miles (700 KM) to the country's farthest eastern mountain range. The project also included developing a new Port where large ships could dock and receive the Ore, plus building the actual mining operation to extract the ore from a very remote mountain range. This originally was estimated to be approximately USD $20 Billion. We planned to hire several local nationals residing along the rail system to create and provide unskilled labor jobs. Due to its limited resources and education availability, Guinea is one of the poorest countries worldwide. An alarmingly large population is uneducated and unskilled, but they still must work to be able to sustain themselves. This unskilled work force would supplement and assist the skilled labor force that would be brought in from outside the country if unable to find the required skills within Guinea.

If there was a job vacancy, they expected to be hired. This forced us to establish a transparent system in a manner that is sensitive to local practice without hurting our ability to get the job done in a timely and safe manner.

As the employees were unskilled, there was no need to perform the mundane steps of checking resumes and background histories. The key was to hire only those people who lived in that particular section of Guinea, but they had to understand simple directions and remain healthy enough to perform simple tasks. We were at the mercy of the local government to issue Resident identification to personnel and prevent job seekers from other areas snatching jobs from the locals. In that regard, each applicant was issued a corresponding number along with their registration. Subsequently, we put them into a bag and took out the winning numbers amid the presence of the villagers and local government officials. In essence, it was a lottery system. As strong believers in fate, they accepted just about any method as long as it was done fairly and transparently.

There are complications and challenges galore in certain corruption-ridden areas like Guinea. In addition to trying your best to mitigate these challenges, you also need to be transparent. Delays and riots are also typically caused by companies showing favoritism. In this situation, we had to overcome the local government officials selling Resident Identifications to personnel outside of the local area. This speaks to the corruption in some areas that the Local Residents will have to deal with and overcome in their method.

Other major challenges to overcome you have to remember, we were in West Africa where many villages lack even basic facilities like running water or electricity. We had to find the best shade trees with plenty of spaces to organize lanes to maintain some order and discipline, which is challenging, as lining up is not a norm in some cultures and each person pretty much does what they deem best. I can go on and on - but to put it succinctly, life is an interesting experience in West Africa., but allows great stories to tell.

We will cover all aspects and challenges of HR, discuss things to watch out for, and tools to enhance your abilities. Let's get started!

1

What do I do NOW????

So, your firm has just bagged a Contract for a project in an unfamiliar or remote area. At this juncture, it's normal for the team to run into questions like, "OK, what do we do now?" You cannot be conflicted and unsure if all you are seeing is the seemingly endless heat, sand, and barren land with no semblance of infrastructure. I hate to say this, but this is not a farfetched, hypothetical situation. Whether we like it or not, projects are not always developed next to Lowes, Best Buy, and Office Supply.

This conjures memories of my stint in southern Iraq. We had limited internet service using only a very expensive BGAM satellite service for only important transmission of information. It was important to send documents to our Finance office to prove our expenditures to obtain funds to operate in the area. Cash was the only way to purchase anything in the area to operate. We needed to scan documents for our main office in Baghdad. The big obstacle was there was no scanner. After reviewing our resources, we decided to use our camera to take pictures of the document and send it across as a scanned document via email. That's one way of being innovative and resourceful. This was the early days of phones having photo capabilities. It was cumbersome at that time to transfer and send photo files. Always keep in mind, you are never alone, no matter what, and the best thing you can do is to know your resources well and understand who is your "go-to" person on-site or from your Home Office to get the job done. Spinning your wheels trying to solve every problem single-handedly can be a frustrating approach.

OFFICE SET UP

Each Department Manager or Supervisor has their unique approach to set up their office at the earliest opportunity to serve the Client. After all, client expectations are non-negotiable. If you are new to setting up an HR office, you can utilize the following steps as a guideline to be successful. Below are some pointers of what most HR Offices entail. Do bear in mind that this is not an all-inclusive list, because no office can be "cookie-cutter" due to factors like logistics, client requirements, project size, facility layouts, and a lot more. The best thing about this effort is that it can be adjusted, when necessary. HR Anywhere does follow a natural progression but it is not rigid about following steps in a particular order.

Following these guidelines can allow your HR team a good chance of succeeding and staying productive.

STEPS FOR SUCCESS

Review the Scope of Work (SOW) from the Contract– Your company has secured a new assignment on a brand new job site. Now, there is probably a new team and an unknown client to deal with. Granted, confronting anything new can be overwhelming. But this is exactly where following guidelines for each job lets you streamline the process and simplify the tasks as you hit the ground running.

Each job comes with a unique set of expectations and responsibilities (do's and don'ts). For each department, there is a separate "Job Description" or Scope of Work (SOW), and HR is no exception! You can generally find this in the project Contract if this happens to be a field assignment with a client. They are paying a sum of money to your company to reach milestones along the way. The Contract can be an immensely overwhelming document comprising several hundred pages of Contractual and technical language that is unrelated to your department.

One important thing is to refrain from doing anything that is over and above the Contract for which your company is being paid. By all means, review the section about HR, but it is always a good idea to review the document in its entirety to better understand the overall deliverables.

Here's the bottom line:

READ THE CONTRACT AND UNDERSTAND THE BELOW ITEMS:

- What is your company building?
- What are the milestones or timelines that should be reached?
- What are the estimated staffing plan numbers necessary to hit these milestones?
- What are the reporting requirements by the Client?
- What is the budget for your Department?

This information will give you cues on exactly what you need for your department to succeed. In many cases, the Sales Team or FEED (Front End Engineering Development) Team prepares these numbers. If you want your department to be successful, you may do well to review the staffing plan's estimate to understand its feasibility. If not, build a business case for additional staff or positions that can be added or trimmed.

If you do not understand the expectations or budgets of your department could be an extreme detriment from the start and cause mission failure.

A good example of HR overreach regarding the budget from the Contract, could be, let's suppose you want to visit local technical schools to commence training for a project. You may have adopted this approach on a previous project or heard others extolling its virtues. But will your company get reimbursed for the time and materials that are to be used in the project? If this is not explicitly mentioned in the Contract, it is very unlikely to be reimbursed. I cannot emphasize enough to read and understand the Contract related to your Department.

HR OFFICE TEAM

A 2014 report from the Society for Human Resources Management (SHRM) suggests that the average HR-to-employee ratio, the number of HR employees supporting 100 employees, is 2.57 across all organizations.

You can modify the above figure based on
- Overall budgetary considerations for a specific department
- Type of project
- Experience level of personnel
- Number of personnel on the project
- What is HR responsible for on the Project?

For instance, a very experienced HR professional may be adept at handling 100 employees with the assistance of a competent administration specialist. However, this should ideally be determined on a project-specific basis and in consultation with the proposed individuals in these positions. The Contract will also identify the client's expectations on reporting requirements, schedules, and type of reports being sent across from the HR department.

The Contract should identify what is the HR Department responsible for on the project? Is the Benefits Department outsourced to a third party or Home Office? If not, a site person or department should be dedicated to this task alone. If this is a mega project or office, then there could be a dedicated Labor Relations person or Department solely for this function. These are all positions and requirements that need to be reviewed and assigned before operations are started. I am going to say it again, READ THE CONTRACT.

REPORTING

Each company and Client requires certain reports or matrix to be tracked on a daily, weekly, monthly, and or annual basis. It is a good idea to be proactive in developing reports on anything that you feel could be requested at any time. There are standard reports listed below, but there are always options for additional tracking. It is possible, for example, that someone might want the daily weather report to be tracked. This is not out of the question and I have in the past added this to my daily "Perstats" (Personnel Statistics) report or daily attendance report.

Some possible reporting considerations for the HR department:
Number of personnel hired
Number of personnel interviewed or considered for each position
Types of personnel interviewed for each position (including gender and race) and the reason for their rejection
EEO guidelines/targets for the project and how are they being met
The turnover target date and the actual stats
The expected daily absentee rate
The duration between hiring request to "boots on ground" arrival

Again, this is not an all-inclusive list though these reports are standardized for most HR offices. Then others may be requested from the client or site management.

If you are not proficient in Excel or Access, it is important to acquire this skill or ensure that you know someone else who is comfortable working with these programs. Tracking easily obtainable and requisite information will be useful going forward. I cannot tell you how many times a Project Director will seek information that they immediately expect and require. It is never a pleasant feeling to admit that you do not have the information being sought, or that it will take several hours (if not days) to get it. That is the awkwardness you should brace yourself for if you do not do your homework of understanding the reporting requirements and expectations from clients, or if you don't take cues from your Direct Supervisors on-site or Home Offices.

Smaller offices or projects under 150 may be able to survive with Excel spreadsheets. If the project comprises over 150-250 personnel, consider buying an off-the-shelf Human Resource Information System (HRIS) program based on your project requirements. For a larger project, you are recommended to buy a more robust HRIS program that helps track applicants, performs more reporting functions, and can feed payroll the required information to streamline the entire process. You may also want to solicit a vendor specializing in this type of software. These numbers are subjective and dependent on the personnel on the project in HR and their experience. It is possible, you might need a robust HRIS system with just a few employees if there are requests for extensive reporting capabilities.

EMPLOYEE CLASSIFICATIONS

After doing your homework and developing a better understanding of the SOW and the type of project being worked upon, you will eventually begin to get familiar with the type of staffing and disciplines required by each project. You may also want to know the different types of engineers, office and field support personnel, and construction workers to bring in. Of course, scheduling is a critical aspect as well.

Speaking of scheduling, one poignant example of a lackadaisical approach to staffing would be to bring a Mechanical Engineer and an example on the very first wave of a Greenfield Project. Besides costing a lot of money, the person would be very bored because there would not be any equipment to install.

A Greenfield Project is normally an open field that needs to be excavated and prepared before the commencement of any installation. This requires Civil Engineers to ensure the area is well-prepared for the type of facility being erected. No ironworker or welder should be brought to the site for the same reason as the Technician or the Mechanical Engineer. What you need are Equipment Operators that can run backhoes and similar equipment to prepare the area. As the HR Representative, it is imperative to recognize the difference between Discipline Engineers and Self Perform Workers.

The engineers would provide the vision and details on how the work will be developed - producing individual scope of work, blueprints, and drawings for each area. The many kinds of engineers required for the project would depend on the type of facility they need to work in. For instance, it is not unusual to have Civil, Mechanical, Electrical, and Instrumentation Engineers onboard, but this can be interchanged with the likes of HVAC, Air Quality, Environmental professionals, etc.

The self-performing employees are often called craft workers. They could be carpenters, laborers, operators, electricians, and so on, depending on the type of project or facility they are involved in. If the project is an ongoing facility and your SOW is to modify or add to it, it would then be called a Brownfield Project. At that time, you may need to bring in Mechanical Engineers, HVAC Engineers, and other similar professionals and possibly craft workers like Iron Workers, Welders, and Millwrights to be part of the bridging process. The bulk of civil work or ground preparation would have already been performed. The bridging process would entail understanding what the project needs, what will be added and how can all of this be achieved without disrupting current operations.

It is all about timing and having the right people on hand at the right time to stay on schedule and budget. As an HR Recruiter, you must work in close coordination with the construction team, schedulers, and/or Project Manager to ensure the arrangement of the right skills at the right time. That is why it is imperative to understand the SOW, schedule, and staffing plan to be successful on any construction site, regardless of whether it is being built in the remote areas of Africa or downtown New York.

I have personally seen this happen on a project in Africa, where someone determined the need for a Mechanical Engineer to be on-site during the first phase of a mining project. The project was a Greenfield operation wherein several miles or kilometers of rail system were to be installed and an actual mine was to be developed. Several thousand dollars were spent on mobilizing and recruiting this person to the site. Upon his arrival, this oversight was swiftly identified when the Engineer started asking questions like, "What did you want me to do?" Since he was already on site, he was "repurposed" on other activities but not effectively used for his original assignment. The project never really reached the stage that it should have before this Engineer utilizes his original skills and knowledge. It was shelved for myriad reasons, but this is a good example of the problem the entire team can be confronted with if things are not planned properly.

Local Recruiting and Training Plan

Mid to small-size Contractors would typically hire a local person for HR roles. They would be unfamiliar with the company's culture or their everyday procedures. It is advised to steer clear of this type of practice. An HR Professional familiar with the company is invaluable to employees that require immediate information regarding benefits, procedures, policies, and numerous other items. This can only be obtained by experience from within because seeking appropriate information within the company involves identifying the "go-to person." It takes several phone calls and/or visits to the Home Office in order to establish a solid contact list. If an employee does not get accurate or expedient information, this breaks down morale and efficiency. Some companies will actually turn over HR resposonsibilties to a Project Admin person. This can be very dangerous and a detriment to project and costly if a major issue arose and not handled properly. Bringing in an experienced HR Professional can be a major cost savings.

RECRUITMENT

An unfortunate realization about recruitment if not performed properly, can be very cost-intensive due to many factors, such as high turnover, excessive absenteeism, poor skills, and low morale, among others. For the above problems, the HR department should seek ways to mitigate as many problems as possible. It is always a good idea to hire local skilled workers due to the cost associated with recruiting and mobilization. Besides being a good community-building effort, it is (in most cases) made mandatory by the local government.

Ensuring that proper skills are in place within the area is paramount. The idea is to get the best-qualified talent as cost-effectively as possible to complete the project on time and within budget. You should be cautious as hiring Locals can be a problem as well. There are always well-placed leaders from the local community that always have sons, daughters, nephews, etc., but be cautious because depending on them can be counterproductive at times.

This happened once on a project-based out of Guinea West Africa. The local Immigration Police were stopping and threatening to take our personnel to jail for not having proper immigration documentation (VISA, Work Permits, Residence Cards, etc.) in their possession. Yes, you guessed it right. This was just a "shake-down" for money in most cases. We visited the Head of Immigration Security to better understand the requirements to stop this harassment. After agreeing on proper methods, he slid a resume across his desk to ask if we could help this person. We opined that was one of those "local investments." In this case, it happened to be the official's daughter, who turned out to be a valuable asset for the team. After some employees of ours were stopped, they called my office for assistance and I put our new local National HR Specialist on the phone. Thereafter, the employee put the Immigration Officer on the phone, and she "explained" the requirement to them. She would also "request" them to meet her in her father's office to further discuss issues in case they had any questions. This always ended well with our employees. However, things do not always transpire so smoothly.

There are varying degrees of pros and cons for hiring locals. In densely populated or remote environments, you're unlikely to find the skills required for a heavy industrial construction project or other similar offices. Hiring locally, in most cases, can minimize turnover issues as many of them are full of gratitude for finding work close to home. However, since there are stronger ties to the local community with family activities and needs, absenteeism can also increase in some cases.

A pro tip: Always research the type of work that has been previously done in the area so that you can decide whether you can afford to recruit locally. This will also help you identify the need to pay per diem for personnel not belonging to the area. This is cost-intensive, but a "necessary evil" that must be endured to acquire the required skill levels for the job. All personnel in the construction industry generally need some incentive so that they can comfortably work away from home, or outside a range that is normally greater than 75 miles. This can be a daily per diem to subsidize for hotels, gas, food, and normal miscellaneous expenses. You can avail many options to attract individuals toward the project, but make sure this is reflected in the project budget. Also, the client must give their approval if this goes against what they have been doing in the past. You never want to "upset the apple cart" with something they have not done before. After all, this could set a precedent on how they operate for future work after the project's completion. The bottom line: ensure that it is handled fairly, consistently, and efficiently. It is only when you start giving special consideration to a group or individuals that trouble always seems to be imminent in the form of turnover and morale issues problems.

A business decision needs to be made to ascertain how sincerely the project champions the workers' cause. It is also necessary to determine whether there is a need to pay a premium or per diem for personnel living outside a reasonable distance from the project to assist in paying for the standard living expenses to be away from home, for them to join your workforce. This client/project decision is unmistakably linked to the overall project budget and success.

Other questions to ask yourself:

Have similar projects been completed in the area and if yes, can that workforce be located and utilized? The Local Unemployment Agency can help provide this information.

What kinds of local Government Agencies are helpful when it comes to providing historical data? This could be Economic Development, Commissioners Office, or Unemployment Agency, etc.

What is the local education doing in the area? Local universities or technical schools should be investigated to determine the available courses for professional and non-professional positions.

After doing some groundwork on the immediate area, extend your search to surrounding communities as well, which could be 75 miles away from the project. That is a safe number that will enable you to pinpoint the number of miles someone might be reasonably expected to drive (one way) to work.

If the local vocational or career center has a construction curriculum, you may want to review the programs to ensure they encompass the type of training that would best serve your own need. For example, it is not uncommon for a trade school to offer a welding program, but make sure they are teaching the correct type of welding for your specific project. In most cases, the trade school might be confined to teaching stick welding, which can be used on a farm or "shade tree mechanic." However, you may need stainless steel TIG welding, which requires a higher level of skill and precision. This is also expensive to train, given that expensive test Coupons are hard to come by. At this stage, get your project involved to deliver some training and material to their instructor to upgrade their program. Most trade schools would not be averse to this idea; in fact, they would welcome it. Again, there's no denying the fact that this makes a good community outreach, but the client must not take their eyes off budgetary considerations.

Most of the electrical training in technical schools might be specific to residential or commercial usage – radically different from heavy industrial needs. The concept mentioned above (for welding) can be extended to electrical or other construction-related needs in the field. One recommendation is to kick start The National Center for Construction Education and Research (NCCER) to get consistent and industry-standard training. Needless to say, it makes for a great community outreach that bodes well both for the client and the project.

The NCCER is an organization that has taken training material from some of the most reputed construction leaders and then converted them into a single consistent training method. This is very similar to how trade unions have developed their training. Previously, a prospective employee would point out that he has been through the training program of Company A. As an HR Recruiter, you would be hesitant to accept their credentials due to the lack of familiarity with their program. By utilizing the NCCER training material, you can ensure the training obtained is validated and confirmed by the NCCER.

Normally, Trade or Vocational Schools in the area or within a reasonable distance from the project can help recruit graduates. Other options could be if a project is long-term that aims to develop programs, consider working with high schools or career centers. This point is connected to our previously discussed point if the client will agree to reimburse. If this is going to be a long-term project with a very robust budget, you can start an after-work hours training program onsite to train local personnel for project-specific work. This can be welders, electricians, or any skilled trades that you may not find locally. Besides emerging as a major incentive for the local community, it would leave behind a great legacy for the company, client, and future projects.

This was done on my first project, and I can recall several people that traveled all over the country to work on many projects for the company. I have personally worked on at least five different projects with some of these graduates from the on-site training program. The project left behind a worthy legacy for the industry and local community, as the participants acquired new skills and used them well to further their careers and the construction industry.

This training can be undertaken at a local high school or career center as an after-hours class, depending on how much space/resource is available. Consider offering after-hours classes to existing employees to expand their repertoire of skills. Doing this can motivate them, as they'd soon be made aware that extra skills are accompanied by higher pay.

Remember, keep looking at the surrounding resources that you may have missed out on. Recruiters do not always have a database of available professionals in their back pocket that are only a call away. The project leadership largely depends on the HR office to determine appropriate staffing resources with proper credentials, licenses, experience, and qualifications to meet project-specific needs. The HR / Recruiters need to be proactive and resourceful to staff projects effectively.

3

Job Descriptions and Mobilizations

Now that you have gotten some clarity on the SOW and staffing plan, the next step is to get the leadership to specify expectations for all positions to the HR Department. This information translates into what we all know as official Job Descriptions. In most cases, managers only want to share details of a title and expect the HR Department to intuitively fill in all the blanks. However, this is not only counterproductive that can lead to wastage of time and money; it can also have dangerous consequences. The hiring manager must provide the maximum possible details of their ideal candidate.

JOB DESCRIPTIONS

Example of a Job Description Template: (Sample Template attached at end of the book)

- Years of experience
- Required education for each position.
- Expectations of the candidate
- Duration of position
- Minimum physical requirements

Typically, each position involves multiple grades or levels requiring different criteria, experience, or education. Usually, this depends on the company size. An inexperienced Hiring Manager could jeopardize the project if he/she is clueless about what they want. Let's take an example to consider an anomaly for someone working in finance.

The inexperienced Hiring Manager could put on the requisition that they want a Finance Representative. This could be anyone from inputting data into a system, such as a Data Entry Clerk with minimal or no experience in finance, to a Finance Manager overseeing the entire department. A candidate for this position would require over 10 years of experience, coupled with extensive knowledge of banking and related procedures. The Hiring Manager would be very disappointed and upset with the Recruiters if they sent a Data Entry Clerk when they were really looking for an experienced Finance Manager.

Let's suppose the Hiring Manager sends you a request for a Finance Specialist with 5 years of experience. They want this person to manage the daily, weekly, and monthly statements for each account before accordingly reconciling them for monthly reporting requirements. If this is not explicitly mentioned in the job description, you could land up with someone who has 5 years of experience in possibly handling a petty cash account. This is a disaster waiting to happen in the form of missed schedules, poor morale, mistrust, and of course, inordinate delays and liability issues!

This also assumes significance for positions across the field, where someone with 4+years of experience in the heavy Industrial Construction Field would be far more valuable than someone with barely a few months of field experience. That is why you must identify each position with expectations as well as the corresponding number of personnel. For example, a candidate might mention (on their application) that they are an electrician. The number of meanings you can derive from this is more than what you may want to handle.

For example, if a project needs electricians to wire up a 75-volt generator, there must be 100% clarity on what that entails, else bringing an unsuitable electrician could jeopardize the lives of many employees on the site.

I have seen applicants who have worked as Electricians for many years. At the first glance, you may think they should be classified as a Journeyman, the highest level before progressing into the supervisory role as a Foreman/General Foreman. However, in all likelihood, they could have pulled the cable for other Electricians to connect to the appropriate panels, which does not need a lot of skill. They may have put in the time in the trade, but the fact is that they have not taken the opportunity to upgrade their skills. For this reason, avoid going by the years of experience alone. Instead, ask, "What have you done all these years?" This must be clearly explained in the Job Description, which is why it is imperative for the Hiring Manager or requestor to fully articulate their expectations.

Ideally, you must develop a project template for job descriptions listing the aforementioned items. The area of expectations must be able to determine the requisite duties. In some cases, Hiring Managers can be reluctant to put what they want on paper. In these scenarios, you can request them to jot down a few bullet items that are non-negotiable requirements. As an HR Professional, you must develop a standard Job Description using an aesthetically pleasing and functional templates before inserting the bullet items from the Hiring Manager. The Job Description must be reviewed and evaluated to withstand legal scrutiny, job classifications, performance assessments, or wage increases, along with numerous other challenges. Again, each candidate must be issued a Job Description that they must sign, and this should be maintained in their personnel file. It is OK to give the employee a copy of the Job Description.

Extending the above-mentioned example of an Electrician to a possible project scenario, let's suppose the employee was hired as a 2nd-year Apprentice. They were tasked to wire up a 75-volt generator but ended up causing an accident. The employee could very well turn around and say they were not hired to do that task but only did it because they were directed by their supervisor. It would be a normal practice to review the employee's personnel file and company documents and industry standards to determine what a 2nd-year helper must be aware of and do, and I can guarantee this: no 2nd-year helper should be made to wire up a 75-volt generator. Sure, they can help, but must not be involved in decision-making or signing off that this was eventually completed. The company would be liable for any accidents that occurred due to improper installations.

That is one useful example of why a Job Description is so vital. Once all Job Descriptions are identified for project-specific positions, you can duplicate them for each candidate hired to perform the same tasks. Updating and revision must happen, but the employee should be notified and sign off that they know what the new requirements entail – this must be done for each spot on the Staffing Plan.

STAFFING PLAN

Note that the Staffing Plan developed from the Contract and SOW, is not set in stone and is prone to alterations, depending on a few conditions, such as a change in schedule that might need the involvement of experienced personnel to get the job done at a faster pace. The SOW or Contract must facilitate the approval process of making these changes on the Staffing Plan. If this is not adhered to, a client could declare that they will not pay for the non-approved changes, which of course, would be very unpleasant for your company.

MOBILIZATION

Now that you have an idea of the actual positions, experience required, and skill levels, the next question to ask is this: Where will the travelers stay?

The normal practice is to review what resources or accommodations are available in the immediate area.

Invest a few days to visit hotels, campgrounds, trailer parks, restaurants, etc. to arrange favorable/discounted rates for travelers as well as business trippers – letting them know that they would be the preferred recommended vendor. Explore the idea of capturing this in normal handouts or emailing to prospective candidates to expedite the process. By having the employee know about the kind of groundwork you have done for them, you give yourself a great chance of developing a good rapport with them, because they will be reassured that the HR department cares about their needs.

As mentioned before, the area of immediate hiring and the expected distance to be traveled must be taken into consideration. If the project's size requires a bigger workforce than what you can find locally, you may need to recruit from outside the area. With that, it is imperative to identify housing arrangements or to have a pre-arranged billing in place if the client has no problem paying for it. On some of the larger projects, I have seen clients buy out Hotels and use them for housing dedicated to the project. Clients have developed land and placed numerous Mobile trailers for housing. There are many ways to solve this problem. The biggest problem is always the cost and associated liabilities of providing housing.

You may want to prepare an informational packet for all incoming personnel that can include:

Available Hotels
Campgrounds
Trailer Parks

Restaurants

Churches

Points of Interests

Active organizations that personnel could be of interest in the area for a protracted period (Water/ Amusement Parks, Festivals, etc.)

The Local Chamber of Commerce or Economic Development Office can typically assist in providing this. If this is a big enough area, they might also have another good resource in the form of the Office of Tourism.

Congratulations! You have reviewed the Scope of Work, understood the type of project being built, and gained clarity on what the HR Department expects. You've also become familiar with a proposed Staffing Plan, the number of personnel needed, and the type of employees that you'll need to get onboard to complete the project within predefined timelines. This information helps you work with respective Hiring Managers to develop sound Job Descriptions to hire the best possible talent for the job.

You are now all set to establish a Recruiting Plan and shortlist people who'll perform those tasks. It could be someone from your team or yourself, in case the project is not large enough to accommodate a Recruitment team.

Good Corporate Citizen

Under this step, you will need to involve the local community to be perceived as a good corporate citizen. This is a hugely significant aspect of the project to mitigate potential challenges that could unnecessarily stymie your work. List this section as local community involvement.

Each project needs to establish a Community Action Plan to identify the local entities to be supported. You may want to do this in concert with the client. By improving your reputation as a responsible business, you will make it easier for the project to get integrated with the local community, which will invariably comprise groups that are seeking donations or assistance for different causes. Here, it is important to funnel this via one office/group (for budgeting purposes) and maintain congruity with the approach.

In this regard, one of the first steps you need to take is to hold a meeting with local Commissioners Office/government entities, as well as law enforcement departments to brief them on the project. More importantly, this meeting allows you to introduce yourself as the go-to person in case of any unexpected scenarios within the community from your workforce. Also, this rightly positions the HR office as the face of the project and potentially helps mitigate challenges in the event any employee lands up in trouble. Of course, not all employees hired by you will be Choir Boys or Girl Scouts. It would be embarrassing, to say the least, if the police show up and publicly hauls someone from the team in handcuffs. If, however, you have established a cordial relationship with the Police at the initial stages, a lot of these matters can be handled professionally and quietly without raising suspicion on the process.

There will be numerous charitable organizations seeking donations or support for their organizations in case of a large-sized project. This can include the United Way, the Little League, or many soccer teams and many others. Tempting as it may be, you may not want to neglect this step as many local employees will be involved in the community and may be able to improve their productivity because they will be assured that their employer is not insensitive toward the needs of the local community. Remember, it's always preferable to leave the area better than what it was before initiating the project. A nice budget for local Charities or Organizations goes a long way in developing good morale and community health.

5

Office Set-Up

After covering everything we've discussed so far in the four chapters, it's now time to do some hands-on good ole fashion HR work, although, as mentioned on the first page of this book, you do not have to follow all these steps sequentially. Think of HR as a breathing/living entity that is as flexible as humans. That way, you'll give yourself a better shot of befriending the process and putting it to good use.

Setting up an HR office is a crucial step, for which you must ensure there's sufficient room for confidential conversations. Have at least one hard-walled office for this purpose and it must be kept insulated from all others to maintain the confidentiality of conversations.

There is no one standardized office set up. Each project will be set up differently due to factors such as logistics and available resources. At the very least, the HR manager must have a hard wall office. This is primarily because they (or any lead person) tend to have a plethora of confidential brainstorming sessions on issues like employee relations, salary discussions, etc.

To prevent the disclosure of confidential information, keep the HR staff separate from other groups, so normal conversation interaction amongst team members cannot be heard easily. It is human nature for people visiting the office to stand next to a desk and become curious about what's transpiring on the desk. They are invariably fascinated by what HR guys do because a lot of it is confidential. Unfortunately, some people get very nosy and not opposed to looking intently at someone's working area to obtain information that is not intended for them. Personnel should never be stopped from coming to HR and discuss issues. HR should be open to personnel, but access to the actual working area should be minimized as much as possible due to confidential information in the area that could be exposed if being worked on. I have seen barriers or a long desk that blocks access to the actual desk area of HR Professionals and the barrier would be the meeting place to discuss non confidential issues. If there is a need to discuss sensitive items, this could be moved to the hard walled area.

My recommendation would be to have glass cover some part of the office doors. Among other things, this would minimize the possibility of false charges of harassment being made against you or any of your employees. Unfortunately, we've had cases where employees of the opposite gender have leveled baseless accusations against someone that they claimed happened to in the office. Needless to say, the partial glass door will mitigate such a situation from arising.

The office location should ideally be located in an area that is not only accessible for staff and employees but can also prevent laypersons from walking into the HR office unannounced. If the project is likely to witness a huge influx of applicants, consider moving the Recruitment office to an off-site office location. This would minimize the large parking predicament at the site and ensure that only dedicated personnel review applications and resumes. This can be facilitated by lower-level HR personnel whereby they can get valuable experience and let their more experienced counterparts perform duties on site.

6

Policy and Procedures

Assuming all things are in place, you should be set to develop Project Job Bulletins or Policy and Procedures.

Procedures and Practices must be customizable for each firm because each client and project have their own specificities, where local laws, locations, environments, and customs require adjustments to Corporate procedures. This requires Project Procedures or Job Bulletins that serve as the key drivers of the project and must gain the approval of site management as well as the client, if necessary. Corporately, the policies could be called Policies and Procedures, but if adjustments are made at the local level, they could be referred to as Job Bulletins or something similar that is recognized by all as Amendments to Corporate Policies.

Consider the following list (not inclusive but is a good start).

1. Project Overtime – What is the approval process and who has the power to approve?
2. Project Recognized Holidays – Are there non-standard client or country-recognized holidays?

3. Work Hours – Cover all shifts, working hours, break, and lunchtimes.
4. Labor and Expense Charge Codes – Work alongside project controls and issue to all new hires.
5. Authorized Signature List – Who can approve purchases/actions and up to what level?
6. HR and Job Bulletin Tracking Log – Admin log keeping track of all JB and revisions.
7. Project Home Leave Procedure – How often can travelers go home and for how long? Who would bear the expenses?
8. Demobilization Procedure – Develop the process to be removed from the project and turn in all company-issued properties.
9. On-Boarding Process – Who is responsible for this and what is intended to be covered? This should include job description, job assignments, benefits, project rules, key personnel on-site, Health and Safety, security, etc.
10. Project Transportation Procedure – Who gets what type of vehicle and how does it need to be used?
11. Housing Procedure – Who gets what type of accommodation?
12. Mobile Phone Usage – Who is issued a company-provided mobile device and how does it need to be used?
13. New Employee and Visitors – Identify areas where they can and cannot go. Who is responsible for them during the visit or initial time on the project? New Hires must be assigned a "shadow" or "mentor" for at least 30 days.
14. Project Dress Code – This needs to identify what is acceptable and what is not for the field and office.
15. Personnel Authorization Request (PAR) or Personnel Authorization Form (PAF). What are the steps to approve, hire and mobilize personnel?

16. Business Travelers – What hours do they work, who is responsible for them? What provisions are afforded to them from the project? What approvals do they require to travel in or out?

As you would have guessed by now, it is possible to develop more such procedures, as the need arises, to cover issues that have not been mentioned previously. Alternately, the policy must be revised for items that are yet to be taken into consideration. As and when Job Bulletins are updated, they need to be distributed to all personnel. In case a change is made to them, it is imperative to ascertain that everyone is on the same page as far as the policy is concerned.

7

Recruiting and Hiring

You've now reached the stage where the actual recruiting and offer-making process commences. Before that, you must know whether your pay scale is on target for the respective Industry. Normally, the pay for a Heavy Industrial Construction Project would be higher as compared to a manufacturing plant or commercial facility due to the fluidity of personnel, locations, and working conditions related to the environment and hazards.

Each company has its own pay scale for each position (as it should be), but this should be modified in specific areas to make it comparable to the pay scales of the area to remain competitive. For example, your firm's pay range may be very high related to local norms, thus setting a wrong precedent for local communities after you depart from the region. Or, it could be too low. For example, you are launching a project in San Francisco or New York, where the cost of living is hitting the roof. Consider establishing a short-term "site adder" to base pay for long-term employees to maintain a responsible standard of living and assisting in recruitment.

FORMS

Next, you may want to come up with proper forms to be utilized in the project. At the end of this book, we have compiled some illustrations for Requisitions, Job Descriptions, Applications, and an Offer Letter.

It is also a good idea to develop the appropriate Hiring Form that would be required from Hiring Managers. This form should identify the following (at a minimum) for the recruiters to understand what is required and to ensure that there is no misalignment of ideas or thoughts.

1. Type of position – Title (e.g. Finance Manager, Pipefitter, Mechanic, etc.)
2. Type of experience – For example, the Finance Manager must be CPA (Certified Public Accountant), the Pipefitter must be Journeyman, etc.
3. Years of experience – Actual number of years expected.
4. Job Description – A general elucidation of the duties to be performed along with the accompanying requirements.
5. Date Desired – Start date of the job
6. Expected Completion Date: Completion of job
7. Pay Rate: Base pay (do specify if this is an Exempt or Non-Exempt position)
8. Education: Degree required or equivalent years of experience in place of degree or trade school certification.
9. The total number of personnel required for each position.

The Hiring Manager should identify how many candidates they want to see per position and then identify who is authorized and skilled to review resumes and applications of candidates. The recruiter should review appropriate applications/resumes that are found to meet the pertinent requirements and forward the best (say top 5) among the lot to the Hiring Manager. This approach adds value to HR by streamlining the process for the Hiring Manager. The HR professional will ensure the applicant(s) meets most of the requirements specified by the Hiring Manager.

The recruiter must also develop a tracking register on the process/path for all positions. Do note that this report will not be impervious to scrutiny and/or criticism. It could also be used in legal actions, in the event of discrimination cases.

The Tracking Register should, at least, encompass the following items.
1. Number of applicants per position.
2. Comments on each application on why/why not it was considered or rejected.
3. Date received.
4. Date forwarded onward or rejected.
5. Track the number of days for which it was reviewed by the Hiring Manager.
6. If possible, it must monitor gender, race, and the geographic area of the applicant for each position. This is strictly confidential and only used for reporting general numbers.

The HR Department should identify someone skillful in contacting candidates for making the final offer and negotiating the proper pay rate for the position. If an erroneous statement is made or a benefit offered, expect it to be followed through with. Worse still, the firm will be made liable for the payment since a recognized company professional is making this offer.

Several years back, I was told that an HR Manager would notoriously lie to employees so as to get them to a site to staff a project. The inaccurate information could be that the project required work to be done for 12 hours a day, 7 days a week, plus per diem. However, upon their arrival at the site, they would find out that there is no per diem and are only working 40 hours a week. The craft employees would stick around for approximately two weeks to get enough money to move onward to the next project; however, that project would get at least two weeks of work from them to fulfill their needs. This caused a lot of acrimony and discontent for all involved parties. It is cases like these that give HR a bad reputation for not being the employee advocate that they should be. However, the industry has undergone radical changes since then and today, information is shared far more transparently.

Without exception, it is prudent to be honest, transparent, and considerate during the process of hiring personnel. After all, you are impacting their lives and they are sacrificing themselves for your company. They have every right to be treated with dignity and respect.

After identifying the right candidate, making the official offer, and putting in an agreement to proceed further, you are ready to hand off the process to the Onboarding Specialist.

After a person has been approved, your Onboarding Specialist will be responsible for all subsequent aspects of the hiring process. They will handle the logistics, communications, benefit explanations, orientations, and hiring process, till the point of handing off the employees to the Department Hiring Manager or Craft Superintendent.

8

Onboarding

The onboarding process is one of the most negligent yet critical processes of hiring. Onboarding creates the first impression of how things are done on the site. The Onboarding Specialist sets the initial tone of the company. Hopefully, this is a positive atmosphere and coordinated very well. In the event there is miscommunication, lack of order or attention to detail sets the wrong tone for the first day.

To begin with, the responsible person must be given proper documents, understand who will be arriving, and issued a neatly prepared Onboarding Orientation.

After the candidate accepts the position, the HR professional responsible for Onboarding should begin communicating with the candidate to assist with the project's mobilization. This should be inclusive of:

1. Project Information Package covering, location, maps of areas, maps to plant, as well as information of accommodations in the local community.
2. Date and time of arrival to the site
3. Location and Point of Contact upon arrival.
4. Duration of Orientation

5. How to prepare for Orientation such as IDs required, lunch provisions, break times during sessions.

Upon arrival, the Onboarding professional would have prepared a scheduled orientation that includes:
1. Site Information – Type of facility being built and some history of the location.
2. Client information - Information on the client and stakeholders.
3. Safety and Security information – This could comprise a separate orientation by HSE and/or security if requested by those departments.
4. Badging information – Type of ID required on the site and the badges' limitations/expectations.
5. Project site-specific rules and regulations regarding parking, dress code, facility usages, etc.
6. Pay cycles and how to submit Time records.
7. Lunch and break times and what is provided on-site or off-site.
8. Key Personnel – List of Points of Contacts with email and phone numbers of important personnel such as HR, Safety, Security, Payroll, Site Management, or Department Leads.

Depending on the type and size of the project, the orientation can be anywhere from a handout sheet to several days of information. Putting a personal touch to it is always a good idea. This starts the new hire off in a positive mode, where they have built a healthy rapport with the project while making it easier for employees to ascertain its value. The person facilitating the orientation must be articulate and well-spoken. Few things are worse than facilitating a meeting with someone who cannot speak well or reads directly from the powerpoint without making any interaction with the audience. In fact, that's one of the fastest ways to put the audience to sleep.

It was my first day on the third project with this same company; it was also the first day when I was thrown into performing the orientation for a room full of new hires because the HR manager at the time had to go somewhere. Needless to say, it was a fairly miserable situation because I was unaware of most things about the project (I was hired to do payroll). I had to read fifteen pages from start to finish and was incredibly bored while delivering the presentation; the same could be said for the audience as well. I vowed never to let this happen again. Within the next year, the HR manager got released for other issues, which is when I was selected to being the best-suited person for the role. This is how I got into HR. It was chosen for me instead of me choosing a career in HR.

The most important thing to remember about orientation is to make it seem vital and interesting. If not, it is a waste of time and you are only checking off a box for the sake of checking it.

9

Reporting

Each project and office is supposed to initiate, update, and maintain their respective departments' reports. The SOW will specify the reports required by the client. The HR department must always be in possession of the standard reporting to be utilized on the project. Very often, you keep running a report but no one seems to care. Then, out of nowhere, a Project Director rushes through the door seeking a report that you no longer track. I may sound harsh, but they're not going to accept the answer, "We stopped doing it because no one cares." If you give this reply, the Project Director might stop caring whether or not you're on the project.

Here are some commonly found report examples in the HR Office:

1. Org Chart – This should at least include the Department Heads but must ideally also include all salary exempt and non-exempt personnel on the project.
2. Staffing Plan or Projection, by department and classifications – This should include all positions that will be recruited with the position's classification and the respective department head. As a result, the Project Controls or Finance Department can give

an accurate estimate of the project cost based on this information.

3. Daily Perstats (Personnel Statistics, or who is on-site for the day) – It is paramount to maintain this report on a daily basis, including during evacuations, for example. It is always looked at when asking how many people are on staff or even on-site on a given day. It is also a good idea to list the daily weather on this for future reference. For quick reference, you can also include personal contact information. Normally, I would have this printed out on my desk, every single day, just in case there's an emergency. It is particularly handy when you are doing accountability during a fire drill.

4. Turnover – The turnover rate of the project is commonly asked during audits or from your corporate office. It is also possible to drill this information down to departments. This will identify whether there is a problem in a specific area or the project in its entirety.

   The formula is as follows: divide the number of personnel departed by the overall headcount of the project or department.

5. Minority and gender tracking per position – This report is a vital piece of information that needs to be developed by recruiting. It proves valuable during any EEO charges filed against the project. Some projects have fixed goals to maintain certain levels of gender and minority hiring.

6. Demobilization dates – Also known as "Demob" dates, these are typically a moving target due to project scheduling and progress, but a date must always be established, and the employee's must be kept informed about the tentative date. This helps retain the human element of the Human Resource. After all, we're talking about humans, who have lives outside of the project. They

should know how long they are expected to work, to be able to plan their lives accordingly.

Again, this is not an all-inclusive list. You can maintain several other reports for a useful matrix. In such instances, a good HRIS program comes in handy that can issue a report on demand without reviewing a gamut of Excel spreadsheets.

10

HR Administration

The HR team takes care of most non-specific employee issues that should be handled by the Department Manager. This non-inclusive list covers:

An Open-Door Policy that means what it says.
The HR and or Management doors will always be available to discuss concerns. In general, the HR Department provides a safe space for employees to discuss issues or concerns regarding supervisors, peers, or any personal matters that could hurt their work. For an Open-Door policy, the standard practice is to direct any employee to discuss issues via their respective chain of command, but that doesn't prevent them from discussing issues with HR. The first question to be asked of them is: "Have you talked with your supervisor first?" If not, it is better to highlight this as the first step. If you feel that the employee is not comfortable doing that, continue engaging them in a dialogue. The bottom line is to have the employee speak their mind.

Policy Development and Enforcement

The HR department is normally responsible for developing, executing, and administering project HR policies that affect all employees. This would include but not be restricted to attendance, dress code, disciplinary actions, performance management, salary administration, etc.

You may want to review these policies regularly to confirm they are still relevant and needed. As policies get updated, ensure that this change is relayed to all employees within the firm. Policies should be made available to anyone upon request either in hard copy form or electronically. As always, the company should adopt a transparent approach for its employees.

Benefit Administration

As a common practice, the HR office serves as the Point of contact for all issues relating to benefit, regardless of the size of the firm. Some larger companies would outsource this task to a third party, but the site HR office should be aware of the benefit plans to give guidance as and when needed and remain a strong advocate for the employee to help troubleshoot questions. The HR professional must be prepared with all important contact points for any benefit-related question available to the carrier or the third party. This usually happens when employees require an immediate response to an issue in the family.

Employee Relations

It is an absolute must for HR to be involved in investigations of employees who could put the company at risk for litigation and violations of employee rights in harassment and discrimination concerns. This representative must be experienced in carrying out the requisite investigation, asking the right questions, or obtaining legal counsel. A badly-handled Employee Relations issue could affect production, dent the morale of employees, and push the company to legal liabilities. To that end, several training opportunities are available within recognized organizations such as Society Human Resource Management (SHRM) to help train the HR Staff on proper investigation methods.

Employee Discipline
This action falls under Employee Relations to assist and train department managers on enforcing disciplinary actions consistently, fairly, and by using proper documentation. This is a vital task of HR to ensure all disciplinary actions are administered consistently and effectively. Terminating the employee is never the intention and the idea is to give them every possible opportunity to raise their standards to acceptable levels. For this purpose, each project or company should have an established process on corrective measures as well. The HR department should carefully monitor department managers to ensure a standard consistent approach is being adhered to.

A wise HR sage once told me to follow a consistent and efficient process at all times. It is easy to get sidetracked in this procedure but remembering this acronym can help you stay on course.

Remember FOSA:
- Facts – What are the facts? The offender will normally want to bring in other issues or excuses on a particular incident. If you are issuing disciplinary action for tardiness, stick to the facts that state what days and how many times they were late.
- Objective – The objective is to be at work at the scheduled time. This needs to be re-emphasized for the employee. If the issue is beyond Tardiness, whatever the problem, restate what the objective is.
- Solution – Sometimes, employees struggle to understand what they can do to rectify the problem. You need to help them understand

the changes that they need to bring about. As a case in point, they may need a suggestion to buy a different/extra alarm clock or comply with a different work schedule or travel a different route to work.
- Action – This would be the time to keep the employee informed that they will be subject to additional disciplinary actions up to and including termination if they do not make the necessary changes.

It is not uncommon for a supervisor to approach the HR, demanding the firing of a subordinate. That's why it is necessary to follow the aforementioned steps to maintain a proper paper trail and to ensure corrective and consistent measures are being undertaken, else you're exposing the firm for protracted, costly litigations. If consistent steps and policies are not complied with, the company will be held liable in most cases.

Salary Administration
There should always be some type of salary range for each classification and position, depending on the size of annual reviews, promotions, and classification changes. All salary actions should be well documented and consistent in terms of approach. The firm must also accommodate Out-of-Step actions when someone is requested to take on additional duties over and above their pre-defined job assignments. If necessary, you can also utilize this step to issue promotions. However, the option must be limited and the annual review period must be used to perform these tasks adequately.

Performance Assessments (PA)
Every employee wants to know how they are doing in the eyes of their supervisors. Therefore, PAs should be done regularly, at least on an annual basis. Having said that, the PA process must not be the place to discuss major shortcomings in performance. Those need to be taken care

of as and when they occur. This is the avenue to discuss areas of improvement or career development and what can be done with the supervisor's assistance.

In many cases, it is difficult for the managers to undertake this process, which, if done well, can be a crucial moment for all stakeholders, including the firm, the supervisor, and the employees. Many managers and supervisors would rather have their teeth pulled out than be compelled to have a face-to-face meeting with their employees and honestly discuss their performance.

I cannot tell you how many times an employee approached me and asked when PAs are done. Everyone wants that coveted pat on the back or honest feedback about their performance. Most people are wired to be desirous of doing a good job, but they also want recognition or confirmation for it.

A great mentor of mine is Roger Ferguson, a tremendous HR expert who we had the pleasure of working within Afghanistan. We spent several hours together sitting in bunkers during mortar attacks. That is when you really get to know someone. He has developed a new approach to Performance Assessments. His book is titled *Big Five. Finally, Performance Assessment that Works.*

This book can be found on Amazon and other locations where books are sold.

Roger managed training programs for several years with two Fortune 200 companies. This novel process eliminates the annual cumbersome and ineffective standard performance assessment programs. This new approach is designed for the employee to establish, with support from their manager- the top five goals that should be accomplished every month. At a predesigned monthly meeting, they will review the goals to determine what was achieved, discuss what must be done to meet the goal, and ruminate on the things that could have been done differently or better. Then, they set new "Big Five" goals for the next month and talk about ways of accomplishing them.

The benefit of this approach is that it encourages regular interaction between employee and their supervisor, thus ensuring the attainment of key goals and imparting a significant benefit to the company. The employee is fully engaged by being part of developing the goals.

You can buy the "Big Five" via Amazon. It is well worth the review and implementation of this program.

Training and File Administration
Some projects might be large enough to have a standalone training department that could be separate from HR. On several projects or facilities, the HR is usually responsible for reviewing with each Department Head to identify what training they would like to implement for their respective department, before teaming up with the Department Head to establish this. The HR administration should be able to track this information and update employee records of any completed training. As and when needed, the HR administration team must update employee files with salary adjustments, recommendations, disciplinary actions, as well as mandatory items such as tax, W-4/ state tax forms, and benefit selections. The Citizenship Validation forms/I-9 forms and any medical references, however, must be kept separate from the Employee file.

Employee Wellness Programs or Activities
HR typically manages any activities and event planning for company-sponsored after-hours or during-hours activities. The project could have a "Project Activity Team" with representatives from other departments to plan the events. Otherwise, HR is entrusted with the task to coordinate project-sponsored team-building events. When possible, include other department personnel as part of the team-building practice. This could

be softball/bowling leagues, weekend picnics, camping trips, or whatever is available in your area.

Federal and State Laws

There are several laws that HR must be aware of to understand and guide the project/office managers on the issue of maintaining compliance.

The federal laws must be adhered to consistently, regardless of the location, but it is also necessary to handle each state or country differently. You are advised to connect with SHRM or legal counsel to keep abreast with the laws for each area of Judicial Court rulings.

While all laws can potentially affect employees, there are a few that must be deftly handled regularly.

- **ADA (Americans Disability Act)** - Having been around for a long time, this law is constantly revised owing to new court rulings. The ADA safeguards the rights of disabled applicants and employees, ensuring they are treated equally and fairly. These individuals might need reasonable accommodations to be able to achieve equal status, but they cannot be disqualified for employment or promotional opportunities if they can perform the same job as someone with the same experience or education.

- **FMLA (Family Medical Leave Act)** – This law is also constantly being challenged and updated in the courts. The basic premise of this law is that any employee is eligible for up to 12 weeks of unpaid leave for qualifying events if at least 50 employees are working for the employer and the requestor has worked for a minimum of 1250 hours with the company. The issue tends to crop up when the firm is inconsistent with application/non-agreement on the qualifying event.

- **EEOC (Equal Employment Opportunity Commission)** – Applicants, employees, and former employees are protected from employment discrimination based on race, color, religion, sex (including pregnancy, sexual orientation, or gender identity), national origin, age (40 or older), disability and genetic information (including family medical history).

11

Demobilization

Demobilization of an office or project is a bittersweet experience. In most cases, it is predicated on the project's success and overall team camaraderie. As areas are being completed, the HR professionals must review the project Staffing Plan relating to the project end dates and issue an appropriate release date notification (Sample attached).

When normal releases based on staffing plan are established, it is extremely important to keep communicating with employees to assist, when possible, for future employment on other projects. This decision can affect their lives, and they deserve the maximum possible notice and as much help as possible.

It is very important to stay updated on any changes in economy or project and client developments that might cause the mass release of personnel. This aspect is handled through WARN Act (Worker Adjustment and Retraining Notification Act) and gets the support of the legal department. The WARN Act comes into the equation when it is known that a large portion of the workforce will be released within the next 90 days. This notification should also be made available to local government officials, so they are cognizant of local impacts regarding issues like housing and unemployment claims, among several others.

HR professionals must take note of all this and strictly follow government guidelines concerning this act.

Demobilization can be an emotionally draining experience for many people. Therefore, the HR department must show sensitivity and patience with each person. In addition to the communication and the demobilization process, the employees must also be given information on their benefits and when will they be stopped. This must be noted on the release notification.

The HR professionals should develop a demobilization check-out form that identifies the process for checking out of the project, regardless of craft or salary personnel. This needs to be sent out before the demobilization and could include the return of any items related to the project, including tools, badges, laptops, or other items owned by the company. A record must be maintained from the very first day on what was issued to each employee. Finally, the checkout process should be in agreement with the original list and continue to get updated as the project progresses.

It would be a project Management decision on how they want to handle discrepancies on what the company shows that was issued vs what was turned in by the employee.

12

Project End

We're almost done! The project closeout can be a dreadful yet vital period. At this stage, most of the employees would have been released and only a few would be left behind to close out the project. What this implies is that those staying till the end might be required to wear different hats or perform different duties to support each other to finish things in a proper manner.

The HR professional should review the company's procedures upon project closeout, including files to be retained and the duration for the same.

If each firm does not have a Projection Retention Procedure, this would be a good time to develop one. However, the legal team must also approve this so that files that could be required for potential litigation are made available. All other files should be destroyed either by shredding or by fire. However, they must not be shoved into a wastebasket intact. HR often includes many confidential items that must not be easily collected by someone who happens to go through garbage bins.

All electronic shared-drive or hard drives on laptops should be reviewed and any files that are not to be retained must be deleted. The IT Department can assist with this process in the majority of cases.

SUMMARY

This is not an inclusive list, but definitely a decent start. As mentioned before, each project/office is different, but some things concerning procedures and their application must be consistently maintained for all kinds of projects. At the end of the day, the endeavor is to develop and maintain a company culture that is consistent to minimize confusion and to ensure alignment of expectations.

When it comes to HR, I cannot overemphasize the fact that consistency is the number one priority. If you are consistently bad, then you might as well be consistently bad on the application of a procedure. The idea here is to be consistently good, approachable, user-friendly, and transparent to all employees. If you do that, you would have given yourself a fantastic chance of succeeding.

It is my hope this book is informative and somewhat entertaining with the multiple war stories. There are many more stories to be told at a later date.

Visit
WWW.GLOBALHRC.NET

You can email me for more information at
Rickefulton@gmail.com

It would be my pleasure to assist any other Highly Esteemed HR Professional to be successful.

BLANK TEMPLATES

Here's a brief list of some blank HR templates of forms that you can use and/or modify from successful projects in the past.

    I. Job Requisition
    II. Job Description
    III. Application
    IV. Job Offer Letter
    V. Verbal Coaching Discussion
    VI. Written Discipline Action Plan
    VIII. End of Assignment Notification

Sample Templates

JOB REQUISITION

PERSONNEL REQUISITION FORM

Hiring Manager/Originator Name:	Phone: Ext:	Email:
1. POSITION INFORMATION (REQUIRED)		

Discipline:	Requisition No.:		
Job Title:	Number of Positions:		
Type of candidate required:	Agency ☐ Local ☐	Staff ☐ Expatriate ☐	Either ☐
Date Required (mm/dd/yy):	Duration of Assignment:		
New Position or a Replacement Position? New ☐ Replacement ☐	Project Salary Grade:		
Location of Position:	Company Paid Relocation: ☐ Yes		☐ No
Amount of travel required: 0-25% ☐ 26-50% ☐ 51-75% ☐ 76+ ☐	College Degree Required: ☐ Yes		☐ No

2. POSITION DETAILS

Expected Release Date or Duration of Position:
Job Description: (i.e. duties, responsibilities, tasks, etc)
Key interfaces (other members of project team, customers, subcontractors, etc):
Job Requirements: (i.e. qualifications, years of experience, education, skills, etc.)
REQUIRED *(Example: BS in Civil/Structural Engineering required; Proficient in ETAP or SKM software required)*
Minimum years of total experience required for position? _____   Minimum years of total industry specific experience required for position? _____
PREFERRED *(Example: Experience working in Middle East preferred; Licensed Professional Engineer preferred)*
Comments: (i.e. Host Country, Local or Visa Requirements)

JOB DESCRIPTION

Job Description of Position	Date:	
Years of Industry Experience:	Education Requested for position: (HS Diploma or equivalent, BS, MD, PHD or other)	
Expectation of Candidate:		
Minimum physical requirements for position: (climb stairs, minimum weight lifts, environment standing or sitting, etc.)		

APPLICATION

PERSONAL INFORMATION

First Name: _____ MI: _____

Last Name: _____

Street: _____

City: _____ State: _____ ZIP Code _____

Home # _____ Cell # _____

Email address: _____

Have you Appliced Before: Yes [ ]   NO [ ]

Have you worked here before: Yes [ ]   NO [ ]

Are you over 18?   Yes [ ]   NO [ ]

Proof of Citizenship?   Yes [ ]   NO [ ]

Postion and Availabilty

Postion applying for: _____

Available Start Date: _____

Education and Experience

Highest level of Education: _____

(High School, GED, College or Some College)

Diploma or Degree Earned: _____

(HS Diploma, BS, MD, PHD or other) _____

College Attended: _____

Certifications Earned: _____

Military Experience:
Branch: _____   Rank: _____
Yrs of Service: _____
Skills and Duties: _____

Foreign Languages: Yes [ ]   NO [ ]
Languages: _____

Employment History
Currently Employed: Yes [ ]   NO [ ]
Employer Name: _____
Supervisor Name: _____
Supervisor Phone #: _____
Can we contact Supv?   Yes [ ]   NO [ ]
Employer Address: _____
City, State, Zip _____
Start Date: _____
Position and Duties: _____

Reason for leaving? _____

Previous Employer
Employer Name: _____
Supervisor Name: _____
Supervisor Phone #: _____
Can we contact Supv?   Yes [ ]   NO [ ]
Employer Address: _____
City, State, Zip _____
Start Date: _____
Position and Duties: _____

Reason for leaving? _____

References

First and Last Name   _____
Phone Number   _____
Email Address   _____
Type of Acqainntance   _____
Number of years Known _____

First and Last Name   _____
Phone Number   _____
Email Address   _____
Type of Acqainntance   _____
Number of years Known _____

First and Last Name   _____
Phone Number   _____
Email Address   _____
Type of Acqainntance   _____
Number of years Known _____

JOB OFFER LETTER

Company LOGO or Standard Header

Thank you for your interest in our company. We would like to extend an offer of employment to _____, for the position of _____ with a start date of, _____. This position has a tentative release date of _____, but could be modified based on project or office needs. The approved salary for this position is $_____.

With your acceptance and agreement, we will initiate mobilization and Onboarding process.

Please sign below and return as soon as possible to respective Recruiter.

_____
Name and Date

VERBAL COACHING DISCUSSION

Name (First and Last Name)	Employee ID #	Date of Discussion
Department / Craft	Position	Location

Supervisors Checklist - The Following Objectives Were Achieved:
- * The Coaching was conducted in private
- * The companies discipline policy was explained to the employee
- * This action is consistent with established discipline policy.
- * This action is consistent with previous discipline practices.
- * The employee was informed this infraction was recorded as a coaching discussion
- * The employee was informed why a verbal coaching discussion was warranted.
- * The employee was informed similar actions will incur further discipline action up to and including termination.

REASON FOR COACHING DISCUSSION

SPECIFIC DETAILS OF INFRACTION AND COUSELING COMMENTS AND EXPECTED PERFORMANCE EXPECTATIONS: (Include possible next steps if actions continue, up to an including termination)

COMMENTS PROVIDED BY EMPLOYEE

SUPERVISORS NAME TITLE	SUPERVISOR (Signature and Date)
DEPARTMENT MANAGER REVIEW: Review and comments for consistent company application	DEPARTMENT MANAGER SIGNATURE AND DATE
HUMAN RESOURCE REVIEW and comments	HR MANAGER (Signature and Date)

WRITTEN DISCIPLINE ACTION PLAN

Name (First and Last Name)	Employee ID #	Date of Discussion
Department / Craft	Position	Location

Supervisors Checklist - The Following Objectives Were Achieved:
* The Action Plan was conducted in private
* The companies discipline policy was explained to the employee
* This action is consistent with established discipline policy.
* This action is consistent with previous discipline practices.
* The employee was informed this infraction was recorded as a action plan
* The employee was informed why a action plan was warranted.
* The employee was informed similar actions will incur further discipline action up to and including termination.

REASON FOR COACHING DISCUSSION

SPECIFIC DETAILS OF INFRACTION AND ACTION PLAN COMMENTS AND EXPECTED PERFORMANCE EXPECTATIONS: (Include possible next steps if actions continue, up to an including termination)

COMMENTS PROVIDED BY EMPLOYEE

SUPERVISORS NAME TITLE	SUPERVISOR (Signature and Date)
DEPARTMENT MANAGER REVIEW: Review and comments for consistent company application	DEPARTMENT MANAGER SIGNATURE AND DATE
HUMAN RESOURCE REVIEW and comments	HR MANAGER (Signature and Date)

END OF ASSIGNMENT NOTIFICATION

Company Header or Logo

Date:

Subject: 30 Day Release Notice

Name:_____

This is notification that your services on the _____(Project or office) will end on (Date). Your departure from the (project or office) is classified as a (Successful Completion or appropriate status).

We want to thank you for your contribution to the (project or office) and wish you well for your future adventures.

(IF APPLICABLE)
(Company name) is responsible to obtain for you a one way air ticket back to your Point of Origin noted as (city), in (Business Class or appropriate arrangements).

You will be leaving (office location) on or around (date), depending on flight availability and transport to (airport location).

There will be required a Demobilization Check List completed prior to your departure to make sure all company items are returned and off board process is completed.

(Explain what happens to benefits regarding cut off date)

Please sign below that signifies our acknowledgement of your departure date from the Project:

_____
Signature   Date

_____
Signature   (Date)
Human Resource Representative

www.ingramcontent.com/pod-product-compliance
Lightning Source LLC
Chambersburg PA
CBHW070817220526
45466CB00002B/690